SIMPLIFIED GUIDE TO MARKETING

KERWIN MATHEW

SIMPLIFIED GUIDE TO MARKETING

PREFACE

This simplified marketing book has been prepared for the busy executive involved in marketing and student preparing to sit marketing exams. The material in the book has been utilized by the author to train business and sales personnel in marketing techniques and students preparing for the various marketing exams such as those conducted by the Chartered Institute of Marketing and the London Chamber of Commerce and Industry. Several case studies are included to challenge the reader in the application of strategic marketing techniques.

Kerwin Mathew, Ph.D., CPM

CONTENTS

1 INTRODUCTION TO MARKETING

Definitions of Marketing

(1) The aim of marketing is to make selling superfluous. The aim is to know and understand the customer so well that the product or service fits him and sells itself.
(2) Marketing is a human activity directed at satisfying needs and wants through exchange processes.

Marketing involves appealing to & satisfying the following needs:-

Self-Actualization Needs

Esteem Needs

Safety/Security Needs

Physiological Needs

Abraham H. Maslow's Hierarchy of Needs

How? Through advertising, sales brochures, selling, etc., by creating:-

(1) Attention
(2) Interest
(3) Desire
(4) Action

Customer ←——————— Marketer ————————→ Manufacturer
(Bride)   (Matchmaker)   (Bridegroom)

Marketing demands the acceptance of consumer orientation by the boards of directors, chief executive, management & employees in every activity.

The marketing philosophy then becomes the major driving and coordinating force of the whole enterprise.

(The **CUSTOMER** is **KING**).

The three fundamentals of the marketing function as a whole must be:-
(1) the recognition & anticipation of demand,
(2) the stimulation of demand, and
(3) the satisfaction of demand.

2 FUNCTIONS OF A MARKETING EXECUTIVE

(1) Directly controls marketing research.
(2) Directly controls advertising & sales promotion.
(3) Directly controls sales & distribution.
(4) Directly controls after-sales service.
(5) Closely involved in product planning.
(6) Closely involved in product development.
(7) Closely involved in public relations & company image.

Qualities needed in a Marketing Executive
(1) Good conceptual ability (foresight & analytical mind).
(2) Good at planning.
(3) Good at implementing (executing & evaluating plans).
(4) Have good understanding of economics, behavioral sciences, finance, statistics, mathematics & operational research.

Marketing basically involves the following (mix):-
(1) Product (planning).
(2) Pricing.
(3) Place (of distribution).
(4) Promotion.

WE CALL THEM THE 4 Ps !!!

The marketer should also be concerned with demographic factors such as:
(1) Social influences, e.g., culture, values, etc.
(2) Urban & rural communities/population.
(3) Family income levels.
(4) Occupation.
(5) Education.
(6) Age.
(7) Sex.
(8) Informal social group membership.
(9) Race or nationality.
(10) Religion.

3 MARKETING RESEARCH

Objective: Reduce risk or uncertainty in marketing decisions.
Definition: Marketing Research is the objective and systematic collection, recording, analysis, interpretation and reporting of information about:-

(1) Existing or potential markets.
(2) Marketing strategies & tactics.
(3) Interaction between markets.
(4) Marketing methods.
(5) Current or potential products or services.

Up-to-date knowledge of market is essential for successful marketing.

Marketing research should supply the following information:
(1) Size of a market for a product or service.
(2) Past pattern of demand.
(3) What factors might affect future demand & when.
(4) Is demand subjected to seasonal or cyclical variations?
(5) Market structure, e.g. based on industry, no. of companies, income groups, sex, age, geographical location and size.
(6) Company's market share, past and present.
(7) Past & future trends concerning population, income, sales, and industrial output.
(8) Overseas markets that present best immediate or long-term opportunities.
(9) Competition, costs & probable results of different courses of action.

* Get information about present market situation and make recommendations concerning marketing strategy.

Marketing Research Data
(1) *Primary data* - new information obtained through marketing research.
(2) *Secondary data* - existing information not collected for marketing research purpose.

Sources of secondary data
(a) *Internal*:- Company's own record, e.g., sales records.
(b) *External*:- Published information from external sources, e.g., agencies, consultants, government departments, professional bodies, research organizations, the press.

Steps in Marketing Research Process
(1) Define the problem.
(2) Specify the information required.
(3) Design of research project:- (a) Consider means of obtaining information.
                           (b) Consider availability and skills of company's marketing research staff and/or agencies.
                           (c) Consider methodology: e.g. observation studies, questionnaires, telephone, etc.
                           (d) Consider time and cost of research.
(4) Sample design.
(5) Construction of questionnaires and/or preparation of briefs for field interviews.
(6) Execution of project, with cross-checking of data collected.
(7) Analysis of data.
(8) Preparation of reports & recommendations.

How to Construct Survey Questionnaire
(1) Questions (and possible answers) should, if possible, be coded for computer-processing purposes to save time.
(2) Length should be kept to a minimum.
(3) Questions to be in logical sequence, from the simple ones to the more difficult ones, constantly maintaining interest of respondent, personal and intimate questions to be left at the end.
(4) Avoid technical terms, vague words and expressions capable of different interpretation.
(5) Avoid open-ended questions if possible.
(6) Provide enough space for answers.
(7) Provide for indications of uncertainty, e.g., "don't know", etc.

Note:- (1) Interviewers should be carefully selected, trained and briefed.
      (2) Include control questions in mailed questionnaires and conduct field checks to ensure accuracy of data.
      (3) Appropriate action if respondents refuse to cooperate or are not available when interviewer calls.

How the Marketing Research Report should be
(1) Carry a title and date.
(2) Have table of contents.
(3) Clear statement of objective of research.
(4) Statements and recommendations in non-technical language.

(5) Logical, comprehensible sequence.
(6) Technical data, e.g., sample information and statistical tables, should be in appendix.
(7) Written in concise, objective, unambiguous style.
(8) Include charts and illustrations if they help present information more clearly and forcibly.
(9) Constraints or calculated confidence limits should be stated.

How to Sample Respondents (to avoid interview bias)
(1) By systematic sampling. (E.g., select 8th., 13th., 18th., 23rd., ... house.)
(2) Stratified sampling. (Concentrate on households who conform to significant criteria.)
(3) Cluster and area sampling. (Concentrate surveys in selected clusters, e.g., particular sales areas, counties, local authority areas, towns, etc.)
(4) Multi-stage sampling. (Development of the principle of cluster sampling, e.g., select large primary sampling units, e.g., counties, then towns and finally districts within towns.)
(5) Sequential sampling. (Complex technique - ultimate size of sample is not fixed in advance, but is determined according to mathematical decision rules on the basis of information yielded as surveys progress.)

How to Collect Data
(1) By observation. (Most commonly used in studies of consumer behavior in stores.)
(2) By mailing and questionnaires. (Most extensively employed.)
(3) Through telephone interviews. (Especially for industrial surveys.)
(4) Through personal interviews.
(5) Through the use of panels. (Most frequently used in consumer marketing research.)

4 PRODUCT POLICY

Product Policy involves both existing and new products and is concerned with defining the type, volume and timing of the products a company offers for sale.

Product policy and planning is concerned with the following:-
(1) Company's total use of financial and manpower resources - for meeting both short-term and long-term objectives.
(2) Kinds of target customers or market areas.
(3) Promotional methods.
(4) Reputation/image of company.
(5) Company's position as market leader or follower.

Companies normally offer an assortment of products for sale, products that come in a wide range of style and quality. This range of products is the product mix. The product mix involves:-

(1) variations in models or styles,
(2) variations in quality offered at different price levels,
(3) development of associated items, e.g. cameras and photographic accessories,
(4) development of completely different products in terms of customer needs, manufacturing processes, etc., and
(5) the adding and dropping of products.

Note:- The greater the variety of products offered the greater, theoretically, is the market opportunity and the less the threat of complete loss of business.

But the costs of development, manufacturing and marketing may be so thinly spread that strategic advantages of concentration are lost - economies of scale may not be enjoyed.

Then again, customer needs may be more likely to be satisfied as they have a wider range of products to choose from.

Products, like human beings, go through a birth-growth-decline-death cycle, the product life cycle.

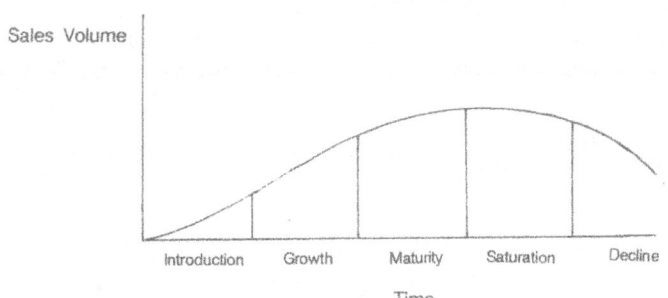

Note:- Dropping products which make little or no contribution can frequently make very significant improvements in overall productivity.

Weak products are costly because:-
(1) They take up a disproportionate amount of management and selling time.
(2) They involve short runs and high production setting-up costs.
(3) They often require special warehousing and transportation consideration.
(4) They incur expense which could be directed to more profitable developments - opportunity cost is high.
(5) They may cause customers to view the company as being unimaginative and technically unprogressive.

Resistance to dropping weak products can be due to the following reasons:-
(1) Management is more concerned with new product development than with balancing current product mix.
(2) There is a sentimental attachment to products which were successful in the past.
(3) There may still be hope for business revival.
(4) Marketing personnel may fear loss of individual orders because of change of products/product range.
(5) Dropping products may lead to assignment of personnel to new tasks, and marketing and other functional personnel may resent this.

How can sales be increased?
(1) By more efficient and more aggressive selling and promotion.
(2) By developing improved products for existing markets.
(3) By offering existing products to new market.
(4) By developing new products for existing markets.
(5) By developing new products for new markets.

What is market segmentation?
Market segmentation is targeting the market i.e., aiming a certain product at a specific market/markets.

New Product Planning involves:-
(1) Research and Engineering, or, Research and Development (R & D).
(2) Plant and equipment development.
(3) Commercial development.
(4) Staff development.
(5) Provision of financial resources.

Sources of new product ideas are as follows:-
(1) R & D personnel.
(2) Marketing personnel.
(3) Associated companies in other countries.
(4) Customers.
(5) Outside technological or scientific discoveries.
(6) Employees' suggestions.
(7) Brainstorming sessions.
(8) Competitors.
(9) Knowledge of government needs.
(10) Individual executives.
(11) A study of unused patents.

Also consider:-
(1) Potential demand.
(2) Product life cycle.
(3) Substitution or product obsolescence.
(4) Market segments.
(5) Sales or production pattern.
(6) Return on investment.
(7) Growth prospects.
(8) Resources.
(9) Know-how.
(10) Availability of skilled or experienced personnel.
(11) Manufacturing problems.
(12) Costs or cost reduction.
(13) Distribution systems.
(14) Patent considerations.
(15) Competition.

Test the market (after Product Development)
It is important to calculate in advance the likely relationships between cost, volume and profit over various time periods.

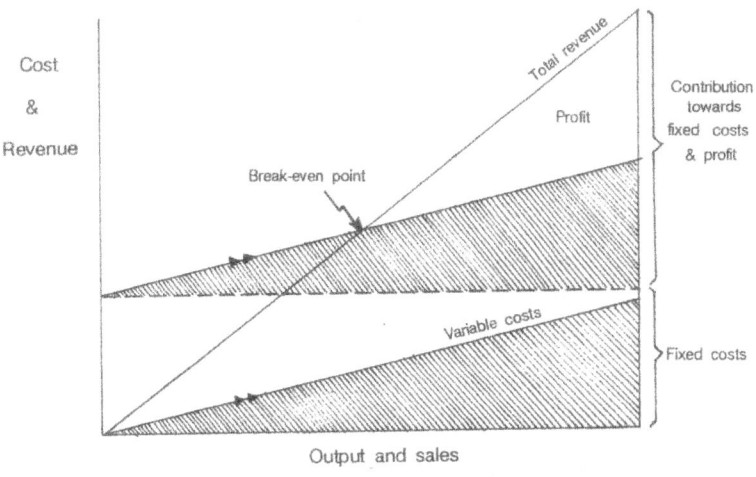

Break-even Chart

Fixed Costs + Variable Costs = Total Costs

Volume of output at which break-even occurs = Total Fixed Costs/Margin of
Contribution (M/C)

= X no. of units

where M/C: (Profit + Fixed Cost)/unit
or
Unit Selling Price - Unit Variable Cost

Product Packaging
Objectives of packaging are:-
(1) Provide protection.
(2) Offer convenience in use, handling and storage.
(3) Provide opportunities for re-use or aesthetic value.
(4) Create favorable product image.
(5) Establish product identity.
(6) Establish corporate identity.
(7) Offer information on product usage and contents.
(8) Attract potential customers.

Marketing Mixes (the 4 elements in their probable order of importance)

Consumer Products	Industrial Products
1. Price	1. Product
2. Place	2. Promotion (Personal selling)
3. Product	3. Price
4. Promotion	4. Place

5 MARKETING COMMUNICATION

Marketing Communication includes media research and planning, public relations and merchandising (in the case of consumer products).

The company has to communicate with the following publics, who are customers and/or potential customers:-

(1) Community.
(2) Educational institutions.
(3) Government.
(4) Trade associations/unions.
(5) The Essential Services Personnel, e.g., Fire Brigade, etc.
(6) Media/Press.
(7) Customers.
(8) Suppliers/Contractors.
(9) Employees.
(10) Financial institutions.
(11) Shareholders.

Advertising
Objectives:-
(1) Informing potential customers of new products or services.
(2) Indicate new uses of existing products.
(3) Remind customers and promote loyalty.
(4) Inform about desirable quality of products.
(5) Stimulate enquiries.
(6) Give reasons why wholesalers and retailers should stock a product.
(7) Provide technical information about products.
(8) Build corporate and/or product image.
(9) Inform public about price changes, special offers, etc.
(10) Explain available technical services.

How does advertising work?
By bringing about:-
(1) Awareness
(2) Interest   **[AIDA Principle]**
(3) Desire
(4) Action

Advertising "pulls", while selling "pushes" - the pull and push strategy.

Public Relations ensure goodwill from all the above publics.
Public Relations activities include:

(1) Issuing press releases.
(2) Giving souvenirs.
(3) Advertising.
(4) Organizing exhibitions and plant visits.
(5) Donating to charity and community.
(6) Personal contact with target publics, etc.

* **Public Relations** *is part of Promotion (Marketing Mix).*
* **Merchandising** *involves store decoration and display, as well as product display.*

Marketing Communication, through advertising, public relations activities, etc., may also be aimed at educating the public, correcting poor impression about the company and/or the company's products or services, reminding the public about the company's products or services, and creating brand/product loyalty, besides creating awareness of the company's products and generating goodwill.

6 SALES MANAGEMENT

Duties of the salesman:
(1) Closing of sales.
(2) May provide display services, e.g., at supermarket, i.e., provide merchandizing services.
(3) May act as specialist adviser, e.g., on installation of telecommunication systems.
(4) May provide after-sales service and advice.
(5) May advise on stock levels.
(6) May train and motivate other salesmen, e.g., overseas agents and retail sales staff.

The organization of the sales force:
(1) Decide how big the sales force should be.
(2) Decide how the sales force should be organized, e.g., by products, by geographical territories, by customer categories, etc.
(3) Decide what is the comparative importance of the various activities of the sales force, e.g., actual selling, providing technical service, etc.
(4) Decide on the kind of men (or women) required.
(5) Decide on levels and systems of payment.
(6) Decide on the structure, such as levels of management.

How is sales force size determined?
(1) The resources available (alternative is advertising, mail order, selling, etc.).
(2) The location of customers and the number of potential customers.
(3) The buying habits and characteristics of potential customers.
(4) The product and customer range.
(5) Marketing policy (selective distribution or widest possible distribution).

How can the sales force be organized?
(1) By geographical areas
(2) By product types
(3) By customer types
(4) By customer sizes, or
(5) A combination of the above.

(1) Allocation by geographical area
    Possible advantages of covering a particular territory are:
    (a) savings in travel expenses

(b) better local and customer knowledge

(c) avoidance of multiple calling on the same customer

Note: Products should be fairly homogeneous and within technical competence of salesman.

(2) Allocation by product and types

Possible advantage:

Highly qualified salesmen can be employed to deal with technical explanation and problems, e.g., stackers and fork-lifts.

(3) Allocation by customer types

Possible advantage:

Specialized knowledge of different kinds of customers, their organizations, attitudes and product applications can be acquired.

What is the function of sales management?

Sales management is concerned with the planning, directing and control of sales forces.

(1) The sales manager selects/recruits his sales team. (This involves job analysis, preparation of job descriptions, interviewing skill and knowledge of personality, intelligence and aptitude tests.)

(2) The sales manager should provide training for salesmen, e.g., induction training for new salesmen, special refresher courses and the like.

(3) He designs sales territories and allocates salesmen to them. Here, his basic considerations are:

(a) to divide work-loads equally,

(b) to provide adequate sales potential for motivational purposes,

(c) to reduce travel and expense as much as possible, and

(d) to provide for simple administration and control.

(4) He sets sales targets and salesmen compensation schemes (e.g., payment by straight salary, salary and commission or bonus, or straight commission, including sales quota).

(5) He directs and controls the sales team (ensures that important customers are given maximum amount of attention, waiting and travelling time are kept to minimum, arranges visits to clients' offices, expands existing business and brings in new business, monitors salesmen's reports, e.g., on potential clients, lost business, or complaints, evaluates salesmen's performance).

(6) He motivates the sales team, e.g., by attending to their personal problems (problems of frustration, morale, being away from home and working irregular hours, etc.). He can also motivate them by, e.g., arranging sales and social meetings occasionally, arranging special sales contests, encouraging positive suggestions from salesmen, sending them for courses, providing equipment and information,

etc.

(7) He makes sales forecasts, short-term and long-term, taking into consideration the general economic environment and outlook, particular industry environment and outlook, the company's and its products' image and competitors, by "guesstimating", statistical techniques such as regression analysis and time series analysis, getting feed-back from salesmen and/or friends, conducting market survey or research.

(8) He formulates the marketing plan.

7 MARKETING PLAN

How is the Marketing Plan formulated?
The following is a way of formulation:

(1) The Environment
    (a) The economy in general.
    (b) The industry.
    (c) The company's market share, advantages and disadvantages.
    (d) Competitors' market share, advantages and disadvantages, new plans or moves, if any.
    (e) The demography of the market, e.g., educational level, trends in tastes, culture or fashion, religious sentiments, etc.

(2) Objectives
    To be clearly stated, e.g., to increase market share, penetrate new market, introduce new product or products, etc.

(3) The Marketing Plan
    How do you mix or juggle around the 4 elements in the marketing mix?
    How do you put the marketing mix into effect to achieve your objective(s)?

The 4 Ps of the Marketing Mix

    (1) Product
        (a) Quality.
        (b) Durability.
        (c) Packaging.
        (d) Features.

    (2) Price
        (a) Low pricing (penetration pricing to penetrate market).
        (b) High pricing (in order to make as much profit as possible in a short time, or, when there is little or no competition and the product is a significant innovation, or, to get a quicker return on investment).
        (c) Target pricing (prices fixed, based on traditional rate of return over a given period of time and related to the extent of risk or investment involved).
        (d) Product line pricing (pricing based on range of products, e.g., selling a product at low profit to

support a product that yields a high profit).

    (e) Cost-plus pricing/Mark-up pricing (margin above cost).

    (f) Variable pricing (e.g., hotel rates may be high in peak holiday seasons and low in winter and autumn).

    (g) Competitive-based pricing (common amongst companies - deliberate policies may be formulated to sell above, below or generally in line with competition).

    (h) Bid-pricing (tender).

 (3) <u>Promotion</u>

    (a) Special price sales.

    (b) Free sample distribution.

    (c) Premium offers.

    (d) Contests.

    (e) Point of sale demonstrations.

    (f) Coupon offers.

    (g) Combination of banded-pack product offers.

    (h) Putting up display materials, e.g., mobiles, stand-ups, etc.

    (i) Advertising.

    (j) Special quantity rate terms.

    (k) Merchandising, i.e., store decoration, shelf-space layout, etc.

    (l) Personal selling (particularly for technical products).

    (m) Mail order selling.

 (4) <u>Place (of distribution)</u>

    (a) Direct selling (from manufacturer to end-user).

    (b) Selling through middlemen, such as:

        (i)   retailers

        (ii) wholesalers

        (iii) agents and brokers

        (iv) facilitating institutions (trade associations, commodity trading exchanges, etc., which do not take title of goods, but assist marketing activities of manufacturers and above-mentioned middlemen)

(4) <u>Contingency Plans</u>

In case things do not turn out smoothly as planned or forecasted, what contingency plans are there, plans to curb the unforeseen problems?

(5) <u>Monitoring/Following-up Activities</u>

What about monitoring and following-up on market ideas or strategies implemented?

Get feed-backs from salesmen, newspapers, journal articles, even friends, customers, potential customers. Watch sales results.

See that things go smoothly as planned. See that necessary changes are made when things are not running smoothly. What about holding, e.g., weekly or monthly sales meetings?

<u>Note the following:</u>
(1) Also mention the sales target/quota to be achieved. Make sales forecast.
(2) Also mention the target market/market segment(s).
(3) Also mention whether to concentrate on local market or to also go into export, or to export only. What about location of retail store?
(4) What about test-marketing first?
(5) What about the number of sales/marketing staff involved?
(6) What about the training and the development of sales/marketing staff?
(7) What about sales brochures/catalogues?
(8) What about after-sales service?

8 TIPS ON SALESMANSHIP

(1) Be courteous.

(2) Be patient (technical products may take months or years to sell).

(3) Be aggressive and ask for orders (without being irritating).

(4) Follow-up by phone or in person after the first sales, visit *frequently but not* so frequently as to waste customer's time and irritate him.

(5) Show your keen interest in doing business with the client.

(6) Do not beg for orders; if you have to do it, do it very subtly.

(7) Ask questions. Help the client to make up his mind. Listen. Do not talk too much.

(8) Try to look and dress decently, in accordance with the client's mood and environment. Do not overdress. Do not underdress.

(9) If possible, entertain clients to lunch, give them souvenirs, such as pens, paper cubes, etc. Try to make them feel obligated.

(10) Even if the client gives an order to someone else, accept it with a smile and thank him for having considered your product and giving you his time. Tell him ever so courteously to consider your product again the next time. Do not abuse him because he is buying from someone else. Maintain *goodwill* at all cost.

(11) Even after closing the sales, never neglect or forget your client. Call him up or see him personally if you can to find out whether everything is fine with your product. Take note of his complaints if there are any.

(12) Carry on the after-sales service, and ensure that he comes back to you for the next order. Ask for the next order.

(13) Check on and ensure prompt delivery.

9 CHANNELS OF DISTRIBUTION

Channels of distribution: Marketing institutions through which goods or services are transferred from original producers to ultimate users or consumers.

Types of channels of distribution
(1) Retailers.
(2) Wholesalers/Distributors/Jobbers.
(3) Agents/ brokers.
(4) Facilitating Institutions (e.g., trade associations, advertising and marketing research agencies, finance companies, commodity trade exchanges, etc.).

* Some manufacturers may however sell directly to end-users instead of through middlemen.

Why direct selling is desirable sometimes
(1) Need to demonstrate a technical product, to supervise tests, to undertake complicated and perhaps lengthy negotiations, or to provide specialized after-sales service.
(2) Lack of reliable middlemen.
(3) Unwilling middlemen.
(4) Product may not be competitive if sold through middlemen (mark-up may be too high).
(5) Middlemen may lack facilities, e.g., transportation.
(6) Customers may be too few and far-between, as in the case of some industrial products, to justify the use of middlemen.

Why middlemen are desirable at times?
(1) Manufacturer may lack financial resources, and middlemen could support him by helping out in marketing.
(2) It may be best for manufacturer to specialize and concentrate on manufacturing (economical) and leave marketing to someone else.
(3) Lack of marketing "know-how".
(4) Lack of variety in product range - it may be better for middlemen to sell product(s) together with other product ranges.
(5) Middlemen, e.g., retailers, can keep stock and sell in smaller quantities.
(6) The market may be large and geographically scattered.
Marketing involves:
(1) Bringing buyers and sellers into contact.
(2) Offering choice of goods sufficient to gain interest and meet buyers' needs.

(3) Persuading potential buyers to develop favorable attitudes to particular products.
(4) Maintaining acceptable price level(s).
(5) Physical distribution of goods, including repacking.
(6) Generate adequate sales.

Channel decisions will depend on:
(1) Whether manufacturer can perform the above functions efficiently.
(2) Cost of distribution.
(3) Profit margin required.
(4) Sales quota to be achieved.
* *Multi-channel distribution is possible.*

What are the functions of retailers, the final link in the chain of distribution of consumer products?
(1) Assist in the physical movement of goods and in effecting a change of ownership.
(2) Hold stocks so that goods are available when required by the consumer, thus contributing to reduction of time separation.
(3) Pass on information of products to consumers and feed back information to producers.
(4) Sell in smaller quantities, i.e., break bulk.

How retailing can be carried out
(1) Through mail order. (High volume sales is possible; shopping-time is eliminated and busy people can get the goods they need easily by post; central buying, more effective advertising and better stock control on part of mail order company.)
(2) Door-to-door selling (e.g., "Tupperware" party-selling in leisurely social climate and ample demonstration of product(s)).
(3) Through retail stores (e.g., departmental stores, counter sales, grocery shops, etc.).

Characteristics of chain store operations
(1) Large volume sales and high break-even point.
(2) Uniformity in the store layout, operational policies, etc.
(3) Concentration on fast-moving lines-popular manufacturer's brands or private brands.
(4) Centralized buying.
(5) Self-service.
(6) Group advertising and promotional activities.
(7) Low prices.

Characteristics of departmental stores
(1) A collection of 'shops' under one roof and ownership, each shop or department specializing in selling a special range of goods, e.g., clothing, furniture, shoes, cosmetics, etc.
(2) Each department normally buys separately, exercises its own stock control and sets its own merchandizing policy.
(3) There may be few economies of scale in terms of supply.
(4) Provide service and convenience to customers under a general "house image".
(5) Provide wide range of specialized goods in one location.
(6) Provide freedom to move around store to view.
(7) Provide special services, e.g., bakery to supply pastries, etc.
(8) Obtain credit from suppliers of goods.
(9) Probably sited in major shopping centers in urban locations.
(10) Fairly extensive local advertising and specialized promotions frequently in the form of special "sales".
(11) May provide delivery services.
(12) Staff are trained in handling specialized merchandise.
(13) Provide house services, e.g., carpet laying, curtain fitting, etc.
(14) Occasional leasing of space for "shops within shops".
(15) Goods may be more expensive than other shops' because of higher over-head and to compensate for better services.

Characteristics of variety stores
(1) Handle a wide range of unrelated goods.
(2) Tend to sell "convenience" or "impulse" goods which are cheap.
(3) Do not give credit or provide delivery service.
(4) Sited in major shopping centers.
(5) Counter service and counter display are available.
(6) Limited direct advertising.

Characteristics of co-operative societies (e.g., NTUC-Fairprice)
(1) Co-operative movement began in Rochdale in 1844 and was based on the notion that consumers should themselves control production and distribution in order to eliminate the waste of a competitive capitalist system.
(2) Dividends were paid out from trading surpluses in proportion to purchases made.

Characteristics of discount stores
(1) Low price is the major appeal.

(2) Low mark-up, with self-service.
(3) Cash sales.
(4) Stores are usually very large (e.g., in the USA, normally over 50,000 sq. ft. and sometimes exceeding 100,000 sq. ft.).
(5) Most of the goods are "hard" goods, but sometimes, there are food and other "soft" goods.

Characteristics of wholesalers
(1) Provide economic utilities of time, place and possession which may lead to economies in distribution - adequate stocks to be available at the right time in a convenient location.
(2) They store goods.
(3) They undertake some advertising or promotional activities.
(4) They fix the selling price.
(5) They arrange credit terms.
(6) They make deliveries.
(7) They offer advisory services to retailers.

Other channels of distribution: selling agents, manufacturers' agents, brokers and rack jobbers.

10 MARKETING OF INDUSTRIAL GOODS AND SERVICES

(1) Capital goods.
(2) Components and materials.
(3) Supplies, e.g., stationaries, lubricants, etc.
(4) Business services, e.g., business consultancy, office cleaning, advertising, etc.

Special characteristics of industrial goods
(1) Product similarity - have to conform to the national or international standards.
(2) Technical complexity.
(3) High unit values.
(4) Irregularity of purchase.
(5) Has "derived demand" characteristic.
(6) Demand for them tends to be inelastic.

Differences between industrial and consumer products

Industrial Products	Consumer Products
(1) Buyers comprised of engineers, factory managers, etc.	(1) Most of the buyers are house-wives.
(2) Careful technical explanation and intelligent approach in closing sales required.	(2) More emotional appeal.
(3) Take longer time to make buying decisions.	(3) Decide whether to buy or not in a relatively short time.
(4) Higher value, generally.	(4) Low value, generally.
(5) Quality is of paramount importance.	(5) Price or location is perhaps more important.

11 PRICING AND DEMAND

What is the elasticity of demand?
It is the responsiveness of demand to changes in price.

What is demand?
Demand is the *measure of the utility* that a product has for a consumer or a market.

When the price of a necessity such as sugar or rice goes up, will demand for it fall? (Inelastic demand.)

When the price of a luxury such as a car goes up, will demand for it fall? (Elastic demand.)

The more a product or general product category is regarded as a *necessity* the more *inelastic* its demand is likely to be.

Besides *price*, *income level* also affects demand.

Elasticity of Demand = % Change in Demand/% Change in Price

What are the factors affecting demand?
(1) Market factors. (Population, income and customer satisfaction.)
(2) Company and product factors. (Company/product's reputation, advertising/promotion and service.)
(3) Demand for other products. (Competition, derived demand and choice.)

Pricing involves:-
(1) Pricing against competitors.
(2) Pricing new products.
(3) Revising existing price structure.
(4) Countering changes in competitors' prices.
(5) Establishing prices for products with inter-related costs or market demand.

Pricing policies
(1) Penetration pricing.
(2) High pricing to make as much profit as possible in a short time.
(3) Target pricing (to achieve desired return on investment).
(4) Product line pricing ("low profit" products to support "high profit" products).
(5) Cost-plus pricing.

(6) Variable pricing (seasonal change in prices).
(7) Competitive-based pricing.
(8) Bid-pricing.

When would discounts be given?
(1) To retailers as margin, as discount off prices.
(2) For large orders. This may attract large orders.
(3) To encourage prompt payment.
(4) When sales is poor or business is slack, discounts can be given to push up sales.
(5) Differential rates can be offered in relation to distance from supply base.

What causes a seller to revise his prices?
(1) Change in cost.
(2) Common agreement as in cartels.
(3) Fear of loss of business if prices are not competitive.
(4) Pressure from competitors.
(5) Desire for higher profits.

How can reaction to price changes be estimated?
(1) Attitude surveys - application of interviewee sampling techniques and field interviews.
(2) Using mathematical models or econometric models.
(3) Statistical techniques such as regression analysis, correlation analysis and time-series analysis.
(4) Use of operational research techniques such as game theory.
(5) Experimental pricing in limited test markets.

Despite price reductions, a product may not sell because:-
(1) There may be a suspicion of lower quality.
(2) Poor product image may be implied (e.g., image of faulty product).
(3) Further price reduction may be anticipated and many may wait for this to happen before buying.
(4) Fear of obsolescence of products.
(5) Fear that seller is financially unstable, especially in the case of industrial products.
(6) Price fluctuations may cause domestic consumers to consider a wider range of competing consumer products.
(7) Prices may still be outside the range of what consumers are prepared to pay.

Other forms of price discount include:-
(1) Free gifts.

(2) Credit terms that are more attractive.

(3) "Trade in" concessions.

Note:- (1) "Price increase" often takes the form of decrease in pack size or quantity, and may not be so obvious to the consumer.

(2) To be meaningful, prices should cover costs, such as for R & D, administration and investment. And on top of it all, should contribute some profit to the entrepreneur.

(3) The more products are seen to be similar, the more likely it is that prices will move in line.

(4) Consider what part price plays in the total marketing mix before adjusting it; price may not be so important to the consumer after all.

(5) Competitive price cuts could be met by temporary indirect offers, a change in packaging or an increase in advertising and sales effort.

(6) Successful pricing decisions are the result of a combination of art and science.

12 INTERNATIONAL MARKETING

<u>What is the theory of comparative advantage?</u>
It is the idea that nations will tend to capitalize on the possession of special natural resources or special skills, so that they can offer other nations advantages in terms of price or special product quality. The theory is complicated in practice by shiftline variables - wage levels, material costs, transportation costs, production methods and costs, scientific and technological development, educational standards and financial and legal problems.

Example:-

Before Specialisation		
Land Area	Country A's Production	Country B's Production
1000 Acres	30 Bushels - Barley	50 Bushels - Wheat
1000 Acres	50 Bushels - Barley	30 Bushels - Barley

Total Output for A + B = 80 Bushels - Wheat + 80 Bushels - Barley
= 160 Bushels

After Specialisation		
Land Area	Country A's Production	Country B's Production
1000 Acres	50 Bushels - Barley	50 Bushels - Wheat
1000 Acres	50 Bushels - Barley	50 Bushels - Wheat

Total Output for A + B = 100 Bushels - Barley + 100 Bushels - Wheat
= 200 Bushels

* To have a favorable balance of trade, a country should not import more than it exports (i.e., it should not buy more than it is selling).

<u>Factors responsible for increase in international trade</u>
(1) Social and economic factors.
(2) Technological factors.
(3) Legal and political factors.

(1) <u>Social and economic factors</u>
    (a) Industrialization.
    (b) Education.
    (c) Distribution of wealth.
    (d) Life expectation.
    (e) Population size.
    (f) Social and physical mobility.
    (g) Urbanization.
    (h) Development of trade blocs.

(2) <u>Technological factors</u>
    (a) Improved manufacturing/agricultural techniques.
    (b) Increased speed of air transport.
    (c) Automation.
    (d) Increased mechanization.

(3) <u>Legal and political factors</u>
    (a) *General Agreement on Tariffs and Trade (GATT)* - signed by about 50 countries in 1948, and aimed at lowering trade barriers. (Members include most industrialized countries, except USSR and China.)
    (b) *International Monetary Fund (IMF)* - set up in 1945 to assist in overcoming currency problems, e.g., maintenance of parity amongst currencies and correction of temporary shortages of particular currencies.
    (c) *Organisation for Economic Co-operation and Development (OECD)* - set up in 1961 with membership of 20 countries, including the USA and UK, and aimed at fostering growth of national income of its members through co-operation.
    (d) *Economic Trading Groups* - e.g.,
        (i) European Economic Community (EEC) - comprising France, West Germany, Italy, Belgium, the Netherlands and Luxembourg, set up by Treaty Of Rome in 1957 - completely free trade

was achieved in July 1968.
(ii) European Free Trade Association (EFTA), comprising UK, Norway, Sweden, Denmark, Austria, Portugal and Switzerland, formed in 1959.
(iii) General System of Preferences (GSP) - to allow partial or full trading concessions for member countries - the underdeveloped countries.
(iv) Various forms of assistance provided to exporters by national governments.

How to Export
Look into:-
(1) Distribution
  (a) Physical distribution of products including maintenance of stock.
  (b) Establishing contact with buyers.
  (c) Providing information to buyers.
  (d) Negotiating sales.
  (e) Providing technical advice and after-sales service.

(2) Specialist Marketing Institutions
  (a) Export merchants (especially for non-differentiated goods such as raw materials).
  (b) Overseas companies buying offices.
  (c) Export commission houses (act as buyers on behalf of overseas companies).
  (d) Overseas agents/distributors.

How do you select overseas agents?
Look into:-
(1) Financial strength and reputation with bankers and suppliers.
(2) Business success or prospects of success.
(3) Integrity/trustworthiness (favorable reputation with the trade and sticking to agreements).
(4) The number and the type of products handled. (An agent should not handle too many products; it is preferable that he concentrates exclusively on your product.)
(5) Business and technical competence, e.g., ability to decide quickly and efficiently.
(6) Marketing strength - size and quality of sales force, quality and location of warehousing and office facilities, reputation with customers, customer coverage, pricing and advertising policies, knowledge of the market and its requirements.
(7) Ability to undertake market research and feed back reliable information on market developments.
(8) Ability to communicate in appropriate languages.
(9) Provision of after-sales service, e.g., stocking of spare-parts, maintenance facilities, etc.
(10) Ability to provide marketing and/or technical training for staff.

In return agents look for the following from you, the manufacturer:-
(1) Readily marketable products.
(2) Good profits/commissions.
(3) Good credit terms.
(4) Product quality and guarantees.
(5) Delivery reliability.
(6) Availability of spare parts.
(7) Training.
(8) Advertising support.
(9) Technical support.

Agency agreements should cover the following points:-
(1) Duration of agreement.
(2) Exclusiveness or otherwise of representation. (To grant sole agency or not to.)
(3) Payment terms, discount, etc.
(4) Rights to additional or new products.
(5) Pricing policy.
(6) Use of trade names, trademarks, etc.
(7) Advertising, promotion and sales literature requirements.
(8) Inventory holding (quota/stock-keeping).
(9) Reports and information exchange.

How to control agents
(1) Visit them fairly frequently, to measure progress and offer help and suggestions (tactfully of course).
(2) Invite agency personnel to your office (for technical and sales training, conferences and exchange of ideas) to generate enthusiasm.

What is Licensing?
(1) It takes various forms, e.g., patent design or process design contracts, trade-mark contracts, technical information contracts, franchising contracts.
(2) It involves the exporting of expertise, involving little expense, avoiding all distribution cost.
(3) It is often the fastest way of entering overseas markets - sometimes the only possible way, e.g., in centrally-planned economies.
(4) Risks are minimized, especially when market is too small or too risky for capital investment.
(5) Problems of exchange rate are minimal.
(6) Freedom of control or domination from licenser on the part of the licensee.
(7) Licenser is also free from any trade barriers that may be imposed by the licensee's government.

(8) Rather than a set fee, almost invariably, the licenser is paid royalties based on the value of the licensee's business.

(9) There is normally a licensing agreement, as in the case of agencies.

(10) There should be adequate safeguards for maintenance of quality standards if licenser's reputation is not to suffer.

What is a Joint Venture?

It is a capital partnership.

Advantages:

(1) Political (favorable treatment in matters of import licenses, taxation and exchange control by host government).

(2) Financial. (Joint ventures are often regarded as the safest, easiest and least expensive method of engaging in international business.)

(3) Commercial (access to new markets and acquiring new knowledge on manufacturing methods or research information).

Disadvantages:

(1) Differences in management philosophy, cultural attitudes, development of plans or dividend policy, etc., may lead to considerable strife.

(2) There may be lack of mutual trust between partners.

Setting up of subsidiaries

(1) Acquire companies overseas.

(2) Start from scratch.

When to set up subsidiaries?

(1) Volume of business expected.

(2) Need to provide specialized facilities, e.g., spare parts, repair facilities, etc.

(3) Strength of nationalistic feelings.

(4) Reduction of manufacturing overheads.

(5) Legal restrictions, e.g., prohibitive import duties, patents, etc.

(6) Capital availability - reinvestment of profits or raising of capital from local sources, incentives from host government, excellent financial facilities, etc.

(7) Good infra-structure, offering advantages to production, in terms of speed and efficiency.

Qualities required in an International Marketer

(1) Capacity and authority to make prompt decisions.

(2) Adaptability, i.e., ability to adapt to wide range of conditions.

(3) Knowledge of languages.

(4) Acceptance of the need for mobility - cannot afford to be home-sick when overseas.

(5) Health and energy - jet-lag problems should be overcome.

(6) Knowledge of local customs, culture and current events.

(7) Tolerance - ability to tolerate people with differing views because their attitudes, beliefs and motivations are different.

(8) Persistence.

(9) Reliability and attention to details.

Look into the following when marketing overseas:-

(1) International "images" - type of advertising, colors to use, words to use, scenes to use, etc.

(2) Participate in overseas exhibitions/conventions, especially when introducing new product(s).

(3) Obtain information/advice from commercial officers in embassies and trade department.

(4) Join trade missions and co-operate with other exporters in exhibition, advertising, selling, etc., so as to minimize costs.

(5) Take advantage of trading concessions, e.g., GSP, GATT concessions.

(6) Export credit and insurance should be considered to protect against:

    (a) insolvency of buyer,

    (b) failure of buyer to pay within six months of acceptance of goods,

    (c) wars, civil wars, revolutions,

    (d) cancellation of export licenses or new export restrictions, and

    (e) delay in exchange rate transfers.

(7) Look at the political stability, quality of work-force, labor cost, cost of living and infra-structure of the country concerned.

13 CONSUMER BEHAVIOR

The process of making decisions is as follows:-
(1) A general or a specific need is felt.
(2) A period of pre-buying activity follows, i.e., an investigation of sources of supply which might satisfy the need.
(3) A buying decision is made (or decision not to purchase), based on results of pre-buying activity and strength of the need.

Every person has the following needs:-

Self-Actualization Needs

Esteem Needs

Social Needs

Security/ Safety Needs

Physiological Needs

Abraham H. Maslow's Hierarchy of Needs

What influence a person's buying decision:-
(1) Advertising.
(2) Displays.
(3) Personal sales talks.
(4) Other people's attitudes and opinions.

The decision to buy is a collection of decisions, such as:
(1) What class of product to buy.
(2) What type of brand to buy.
(3) What is the design desired.
(4) What quantity to buy.
(5) Where to buy from.
(6) Whom to buy from.
(7) At what price to buy at.

(8) What payment terms to buy at.

* *Uncertainty and delay in buying is often the result of conflict between rational economic motives and non-rational external and internal stimuli. "Impulse" buying is more frequently found where there is no economic anxiety, with comparatively inexpensive, frequently purchased products, e.g., where non-rational external stimuli (packaging, promotions, display, etc.) have a major influence.*

The influence of personality and environment on buying decisions
(1) Personal aspirations.
(2) Temperament and philosophy.
(3) Cultural and organizational influence, e.g., cultural values.
(4) Urban and rural communities.
(5) Family income levels.
(6) Occupations.
(7) Education.
(8) Age.
(9) Sex.
(10) Informal social group membership.
(11) Race or nationality.
(12) Religion.
(13) Other socio-economic factors, such as reputation of store, etc.
(14) The image and reliability of the seller.
(15) How the customer perceives that the product can satisfy his needs, e.g., systems selling, i.e., selling a product that incorporates several functions. (He wants value for his money.)

How does a customer make a buying decision?
The process is as follows:

	AIDA Principle
(1) Awareness (of product)	Awareness
(2) Knowledge	Interest
(3) Liking	Desire
(4) Preference	Action
(5) Conviction	
(6) Purchase	

<u>What is Product Positioning? (Also a pricing strategy.)</u>
Product positioning is the targeting of products, with specific price ranges, at specific markets.

For example, the Toyota Starlet with a specific affordable price is aimed at clerks and secretaries, the Toyota Corolla at middle level executives and managers, and the Toyota Cressida at senior managers and bosses.

<u>Where to advertise for the following:-</u>

(a) <u>Consumer Products</u>
   (i)   Newspapers
   (ii)   Magazines
   (iii) Women's journals
   (iv) Mass media such as TV and cinema
   (v)   Yellow pages of telephone directory
   (vi) Bus panels
   (vii) Sign boards and posters

(b) <u>Industrial Products</u>
   (i)   Technical journals
   (ii) Trade directories
   (iii) Yellow pages of telephone directory

14 CASE STUDY

(1) You are the Business Manager of a big emporium group, XYZ Corporation, which specializes in consumer products. As the business manager for the group, you are responsible for all marketing, merchandising and public relations matters within the corporation.

One day, the group Managing Director asked you to pop in to discuss the possibility of setting up a departmental store in Newtown Housing Estate with him.

After the three-hour discussion, you are asked to submit plans and proposals for the new departmental store in Newtown within the next few days or so.

As the Business Manager for the group, what are your plans and proposals for this new departmental store?

(2) Dowell Pte. Ltd. sells engineering tools to various industries in the country. You, as the Marketing Manager of Dowell, is responsible for all marketing and sales activities within the company.

One day, the Managing Director called you into his office to discuss the current market situation in the country. The Managing Director is concerned about the shrinking market share for the company's tools.

As the Marketing Manager of Dowell, you are asked to account for the company's shrinking market share, to increase the market share of the company's products in the country, and to devise plans to introduce the products into one of the ASEAN countries, where the market potential is great.

Give your plans as to how to increase the market share of your tools in the country and how you are going to penetrate an ASEAN market which has great potential.

www.ingramcontent.com/pod-product-compliance
Lightning Source LLC
Chambersburg PA
CBHW081754170526
45167CB00009B/4021